UNSOLVED MYSTERIES

HAUNTED HOUSES

BY JAMIE KALLIO

The
Child's
World®

ABOUT THE AUTHOR

Jamie Kallio is a youth services librarian
and author of many nonfiction books for
children. She once lived in a house that
might have been haunted.

Published by The Child's World®
1980 Lookout Drive • Mankato, MN 56003-1705
800-599-READ • www.childsworld.com

ACKNOWLEDGMENTS
The Child's World®: Mary Berendes, Publishing Director
Red Line Editorial: Editorial direction
The Design Lab: Design
Amnet: Production

DESIGN ELEMENT: Shutterstock Images

PHOTOGRAPHS ©: Shutterstock Images, cover, 12; Iriana Shiyan/
Shutterstock Images, 6; Anki Hoglund/iStockphoto, 8; Everett Historical/
Shutterstock Images, 13; iStockphoto, 15; Jessica Rinaldi/Reuters/
Corbis, 18; S. W. Fallis/Library of Congress, 20; Chris Mueller/
iStockphoto, 23

ISBN 9781634070744
LCCN 2014959761

Printed in the United States of America
Mankato, MN
July, 2015
PA02266

TABLE OF CONTENTS

CHAPTER ONE

STRANGE FOOTSTEPS AND GHOSTLY SIGHTS

It was an early spring morning in 1960. June Reading had just entered the Whaley House. This house was very old and beautiful. But it needed repairs. Few people had been there since 1953. The San Diego Historical Society was fixing it up. They were turning the house into a museum. People could visit to learn about the past. Reading was leading the project.

Suddenly, Reading heard footsteps upstairs. She checked every room. No one was there. Soon, she returned to her work. Yet she still heard footsteps. Other historians and repair workers said they heard the footsteps, too. No one could explain the odd sound. Was there a ghost in the house?

The Whaley House soon opened as a museum. But the footsteps continued. Visitors and workers heard other strange noises. Some said they heard loud laughter. Others reported hearing organ music. They heard the sounds even when they were alone in the house. Some people also saw ghostly figures.

Today, the Whaley House is known as the most haunted house in the United States. More than 125,000 people visit the house each year. Many visitors report seeing or hearing people who aren't really there. To this day, visitors hear eerie footsteps upstairs.

People say the house is haunted because of its sad history. In 1856, the Whaley family purchased land in California. The land had once held a courthouse and jail.

Some Whaley House visitors say they have seen Anna Whaley in this room.

Some criminals had died there. One criminal was called Yankee Jim. He was a tall man who wore very heavy boots.

Thomas Whaley built the house in 1857. He said that he often heard footsteps in the house. He believed Yankee Jim's ghost lived there. Some people think Yankee Jim still haunts the Whaley House. They say his ghost is angry. Other ghosts have also been reported. Visitors think they have seen the ghosts of Thomas Whaley and his wife, Anna. Some even say they have seen the ghost of the Whaleys' dog.

People have reported similar sights and sounds in other places. They hear eerie footsteps or see shadowy figures. Millions of Americans believe that some houses are haunted. They think ghosts cause the mysterious events. **Skeptics** believe there is another explanation. But many questions remain about these strange places.

What Is a Haunted House?

If a house is truly haunted, it is said to contain **paranormal** activity. That means that ghosts, or spirits, are in the house. Ghosts might be people who once lived there. People who study haunted houses are called paranormal **investigators**. Most paranormal investigators believe the spirit of a dead person can haunt a house.

Hauntings are often reported in very old houses. People hear strange noises and even voices in these places. Objects may seem to move by themselves. Lights can mysteriously flicker and go off. Unexplained smells can fill a room. Someone may see an **apparition**. An apparition is the filmy shape of a person. People have also reported apparitions of animals.

An apparition is a faint or filmy shape of a person or animal.

Skeptics have other explanations for these events. Creaking noises are common in old houses. They can occur naturally. People might be mistaken about what they see or smell. Some may only dream about ghosts.

There is no clear proof that some houses are haunted. But many people believe they are. Researchers are trying to learn the truth.

MYTH OR FACT?

Scientists have investigated possible haunted places.

This is a fact. In 2005, scientists in Scotland brought volunteers to different locations. Some of the places were considered haunted. Other places were not considered haunted. The volunteers did not know which places were which. People who visited the "haunted" locations were more likely to report feeling strange or scared.

CHAPTER TWO

HAUNTED PLACES AROUND THE WORLD

People have believed in haunted houses for thousands of years. One of the oldest stories of a haunted place is from about 470 BC. Pausanias was a general from the ancient city of Sparta. He was accused of betraying his city. Pausanias was imprisoned in the Temple of Athena. He died in the temple. Later, people claimed that terrible noises came from the temple. They feared the ghost of Pausanias.

Not all ancient ghosts were considered scary. Many **cultures** believed in house spirits. These spirits were thought to protect a family's **fortune**. People had different ways of honoring the house spirits. Some set out food for them. Others used paintings or small statues to honor them.

Many cultures viewed the spirits as ghosts. Others thought of them as fairies or gods. Legends say that house spirits helped people. They could pinch or scratch a lazy person. Happy spirits would watch over families. The spirits would warn families of danger by banging dishes or exciting pets.

Some cultures still believe in house spirits. In Thailand, many homes have tiny houses in their yards. These are called spirit houses. They are meant to honor ancestors who have died. People light candles in the spirit houses. Sometimes, they bring offerings of food. They want to keep their ancestors happy. They believe that if their ancestors are happy, the ancestors will help the family. If the spirits are unhappy, the family will fall on bad fortune.

Thai spirit houses are often mounted on posts in yards.

Famous American Haunted Houses

Few Americans today believe in house spirits. But many believe that certain houses are haunted. One famous example is the White House. Several presidents have reported seeing ghosts there. Visitors say that President Abraham Lincoln's ghost paces the floors. Sometimes, he sits or looks out of windows. Some people have reported seeing First Lady Abigail Adams hanging laundry. Presidents and their families have heard strange sounds at night.

Abigail Adams was the First Lady of the United States from 1797 to 1801.

Many reports of haunted houses are from the southern United States. One famous place is the Gainesville mansion in Alabama. In the 1840s, Evelyn Carter was a servant in the home. She looked after the children. Often, she played the piano and sang. Carter died of an illness. Cold weather delayed her burial. Some say that the delay angered her spirit. People say that they often hear unexplained piano music in the house. They think the sounds are from Carter's spirit.

MYTH OR FACT?

There was a haunted house in Amityville, New York.

*This is a myth. In 1977, the Lutz family bought an old house in Amityville, New York. They lived there for only 28 days. They reported eerie voices, music, and footsteps. They said an evil spirit talked to their daughter. Filmmakers made a movie of their story. Later, people found out that the haunting was a **hoax**. The Lutzes invented the events.*

Other Haunted Places

Not all hauntings happen in houses. Many old asylums, prisons, and castles have ghost stories. Often, they are places with a sad history.

The Trans-Allegheny Lunatic Asylum was built in West Virginia in 1858. It was only big enough to hold 250 patients. By 1950, the asylum had more than 2,000 patients. It was very crowded. Some patients were treated poorly. Many died in the asylum.

The asylum is now closed. But some people believe that ghosts of former patients still live there. Visitors to the asylum have reported seeing apparitions. They have also heard screams and voices. Some see flickering lights. One reported ghost is a girl named Lily. Visitors say that she plays with a ball. They think that Lily is lonely. Often, she asks guests questions.

Many famous haunted places are popular tourist spots. People are curious about them. They want to know if the places are really haunted.

This is a myth. Some highways and cemeteries are said to be haunted. In 1817, a family in Adams, Tennessee, said that a witch haunted their cabin. Later, the cabin was torn down. Some believe the witch still haunts a nearby cave.

Many people believe that the West Virginia Penitentiary, a prison, is haunted.

CHAPTER THREE

EXPLAINING HAUNTED HOUSES

What causes some houses to seem haunted? No one really knows. People have different ideas. Some explanations are scientific. Others are paranormal.

Paranormal Explanations

If ghosts exist, why are they here? There are many guesses. Perhaps ghosts do not realize they are dead. Or they may have unfinished business. They could want to communicate with the living. Some ghosts might be angry. They may want revenge

Paranormal investigators use equipment to try to locate a ghost.

for events from the past. In some cases, a spirit may not have been buried properly.

Some researchers think that ghosts stay in places where bad things happened. They say a house soaks up "emotional energy." This energy comes from the feelings of people who lived there. When new people move in, the energy causes a haunting. Ghosts of people who lived in the house appear.

Sometimes, families call for help with haunted houses. They might call in a person who claims to talk to the dead. This person might ask the ghost what it wants. Ghost hunters have equipment to help them track down ghosts. This equipment includes video cameras, thermometers, compasses, and **Geiger counters**.

Ghost hunters believe that ghosts cause changes in their surroundings. They use the equipment to measure any changes in the environment. They also try to capture video or audio recordings of the spirits. Ghost hunters hope to rid the house of spirits. They try to find what caused the haunting. Then they try to convince the ghosts to leave.

Scientific Explanations

Skeptics have other explanations for haunted houses. Strange noises are common in old buildings. Pipes may rattle against floors. Door hinges might rust and creak. Sometimes, mice or other animals live in the walls. These animals can make noise. They can also cause pets to act strangely. Cold spots might be from the wind. In old houses, cold drafts can enter through holes or cracks.

What about people who see apparitions? Most ghost sightings are reported late at night or early in the morning. Skeptics think some people suffer from "sleep paralysis." In this stage of sleep, people cannot move. They are very sleepy. They might even still be dreaming. In this state, they think they see apparitions. The apparitions are actually **hallucinations** or dreams.

Another explanation involves carbon monoxide, a type of gas. The air has small amounts of carbon monoxide. But larger amounts of this gas are poisonous. Carbon monoxide can enter homes through faulty heaters and fireplaces. Breathing carbon monoxide can cause hallucinations. Perhaps this gas makes people believe a house is haunted.

People have created hoaxes about ghosts. They might invent stories to gain fame. Some hoaxers take advantage of others' grief. In the 1800s, William Mumler called himself

MYTH OR FACT?
Nearly half of all Americans believe in ghosts.

This is a fact. Skeptics say there is no **evidence** that ghosts exist. But many Americans disagree. Almost half of Americans say they believe in ghosts. About one in five Americans say they have seen a ghost.

The faces of ghosts seemed to appear in spirit photographs.

a "spirit photographer." He told families that he could photograph ghosts. People bought his pictures of their loved ones who had died. But the photographs didn't really show ghosts. Mumler made them by combining different images. He knew the fake photographs would comfort people. Mumler made money from grieving families. Some other people sold similar photographs.

Remaining Questions

Some people today say they can contact ghosts. Skeptics think these people are hoaxers like Mumler. Yet millions of people believe spirits can visit the living. Many also believe that these spirits haunt houses or other places. Some are scared of ghosts. Others are comforted by the idea that loved ones are not really gone.

Haunted houses have a long history. Scientists want to study them further. They want to know what happens when people think they see ghosts. Perhaps soon we will understand more about the strange events in old houses.

Glossary

apparition (ap-uh-RISH-un) An apparition is a ghost or spirit of a dead person. Some people say they have seen an apparition of Thomas Whaley.

cultures (KUL-churz) Cultures are the traditions of certain groups of people. In many cultures, people tell stories about haunted houses.

evidence (EV-uh-dehnss) Evidence is a fact or example that shows an idea is true. Some people say there is not enough evidence that houses can be haunted.

fortune (FOR-chuhn) A person's fortune is what happens to the person in the future. Some people believe that house spirits control a family's fortune.

Geiger counters (GUY-gur COWN-turz) Geiger counters are tools that measure radiation levels in an area. Ghost hunters think that Geiger counters help them find ghosts.

hallucinations (huh-loo-sun-NAY-shunz) Hallucinations are things a person sees that are not really there. Ghost sightings may be hallucinations.

hoax (HOHKS) A hoax is a trick or practical joke. William Mumler's spirit photography business was a hoax.

investigators (in-VESS-tih-gate-orz) Investigators are people who research or study a certain topic. Paranormal investigators study haunted houses and ghosts.

paranormal (pa-ruh-NOR-mal) When something is paranormal, it cannot be explained by science. Haunted houses and ghosts are paranormal.

skeptics (SKEP-tiks) Skeptics are people who doubt an idea or explanation. Skeptics do not believe that ghosts exist.

To Learn More

BOOKS

Brucken, Kelli M. *Haunted Houses.* San Diego: KidHaven, 2006.

Stone, Adam. *The Unexplained: Haunted Houses.* Minneapolis: Bellwether, 2012.

Williams, Dinah. *Dark Mansions.* New York: Bearport, 2012.

WEB SITES

Visit our Web site for links about haunted houses: **childsworld.com/links**

*Note to Parents, Teachers, and Librarians: We routinely verify our Web links to make sure
they are safe and active sites. So encourage your readers to check them out!*

Index